UP FROM UNDERNEATH

PRESTON POSKEY

MILTON & HUGO L.L.C.
4407 Park Ave., Suite 5
Union City, NJ 07087, USA

Website: *www. miltonandhugo.com*
Hotline: *1- 888-778-0033*
Email: *info@miltonandhugo.com*

Ordering Information:
Quantity sales. Special discounts are granted to corporations, associations, and other organizations. For more information on these discounts, please reach out to the publisher using the contact information provided above.

Library of Congress Control Number: 2024902707
ISBN-13:   979-8-89285-029-2   [Paperback Edition]
                  979-8-89285-030-8   [Digital Edition]

Rev. date: 01/25/2024

To Eliana and Preston, you motivate me more than you know.

To Carla Saunders, and Jessica Poskey, thank you both for listening when needed.

In memory of Henry Poskey, I could not have asked for a better father.

Special thanks to Randy Plym for reading, re-reading and providing valuable insight.

Contents

Introduction

If you are reading this, then we have both come further than I ever thought we would. I have written for over 25 years, but I could never move forward with publishing anything. I was always overcritical, and I would second guess myself. Dear reader, if there is something you enjoy doing, I would advise you to pursue it completely and passionately. Perhaps there is more work to be done, but pursue it wholeheartedly – you never know where you could end up.

Hemmingway once said writing was easy, all one needed to do was sit in front of a typewriter and bleed. I think that this work encapsulates that idea. I have used these poems and this canvas to work through coming up from underneath the weight of my world crumbling. In these pages you will find works and words that are seemingly contradictory. They are and they are not. This is a snapshot of emotions and ideas and during this time those were ever-changing. I hope you enjoy this work; I hope that you can connect with these words and know that you are not alone. I hope that this work finds you well, or at least on the path to wellness.

Sincerely,
Preston Poskey

My Life Will Be Alive

Surely life is not without pain, which is why it must be
fully grasped.
'Tis not for me to wonder at what time the painful
arrow flies,
for when it strikes my side, I must be full, so full that
even the ocean wide dare not chide the river flowing
from my side.

No, I will not recede as does the tide,
For half measures never reveal treasures.

Yea, for this and this alone, I will live,
and my life will be alive with celebration!

When Betrayal's arrow is knocked and cocked,
I will stand motionless.
I will wait and it will strike flesh and bone.
I will bleed tears and my wound will haunt you at the
stopping of our clocks.
I love without fear; my love has no locks.

Come and Go

You move underneath,
painfully quiet–
building urgency,
subsiding,
rising again.

You are a tide that comes and goes.
I summon, you refuse.
You call, I will not receive you.

Go then into the thicket,
heavy with madness.
Go then into the mountains,
rise as volcanic ash.
Go then into my being,
cut yourself on my unabashed need.

Fear not,
return to me in fullness.
Fear not,
fly from me fit to strike.

What is Man?

Of what importance is man?
That strange creature who paints with colors he cannot
understand.
Alone a roaring lion, yet in the streets he bleats like a
lamb.

Such comic tragedies are surely beyond Shakespeare's
stride.
Oh God, in you bountiful humor must abide!

Poem for a Friend

I have heard it was written in stone and sand
that woman was formed with the bones of man.
For this, I say with certainty,
She is not of you!

While I dare not say she is of me,
I can say with clarity-
She is not of you!

What Measure?

Is it right to tow a feathered heart back to land?
Could I be content to watch wide eyed
and listen to the subtle hymns?

Or should I pull it down from heavenly heights
for the joy of holding in hand
a songstress from distant dusty lands?

Would my hovering hand become a smothering band
for such a thing as was always meant to fly?

A Lullaby/ A Father's Prayer

A day soon to end.
Midnight come quick,
work your gentle trick.
This consciousness bend sweetly to sleep

Wherever she may be,
touch her heart with sweet dreams
of soft and fluffy things.
Let Night's gentle kiss
show her she is dearly missed.

I Wish I Could Write

I wish I could write
of valleys and rivers,
but tonight my sadness bleeds through
every line every hue—
dark and hard.

If I could borrow something,
some strange concoction
to lighten this dreary shade.

I wish I could write of love's first kiss,

but there are these two brown haired angels that I miss.
Their names are seared in all the corners of my brain.

Heart Strung

She strung my heart like a guitar.
Steel strings wound and pulled through,
soft palpating bruise.
Feel it come alive,
Sweet reverberating blues.

Where Shall My Passion Lie?

On which road will my passion lie?
This I ask whilst running from this to that
and that to this again.
I wonder then,
why must it lie at all?

Above the air is thinner,
the obstacles fewer yet.
Yes, I'll bet
few have really let their passion fly!

Who Then?

*Consciousness must stir and defend the inspiration that
intuition found.
Let failing eyes see what love feels, and understand what
words cannot fathom.
Time, stir your withered hand,
defend innocent dreams.*

*Justice glimmers,
just out of reach.
Is there no plan?
No Superman?
Who then will defend sheepish love from the wolf's
bloodthirsty tongue?*

Hope is Light

Night yawns and swallows secrets,
Sleep spawns forgetfulness.
Time bemoans remembered regrets,
cast like jagged stones into the subconscious.

Trembling light flickers, surrounded.
Tiny quaking might leaves the lonesome dark
confounded.
Truth's secret fractured and compounded,
a candle's light was never meant for bright spaces.

Carving Symbols on Your Bones

If I could move you
I would call you home
and whisper while carving symbols on your bones,
Language archaic,
buried underneath your starlit mosaic.

If we could remember hours spent lakeside
admiring the frozen tide,
I would whisper while carving symbols on your bones.

My traveled soul,
my unraveled soul
knows not home

Years stretched and sewn apart
Thread lost from Time's spools
If you would touch this broken heart
I would whisper while carving symbols on your bones.

Twilight Life

Bathed in twilight
drawn in lines of blood and fear.
When I think I know,
I know I don't know who I am.
Drink me in and take my hand.
Stars are born and worlds dead,
sail me away on seas of illusory dreams.
Sweet Amnesia, take me in your formless arms
Smiles choking back the screams of tiny dying hearts.
Porcelain painted masks of obligation.

Just hold me, looking at the sky,
brushed with pastel blue, purpled bruises, and auburn explosions,
Sun drowned horizon.
Bring the dark cool indifferent acceptance,
shadows that do not show tears
carving lines in this dirt life.

In the soft black dancing shadows, could we discover trust?
Find me walking on your water,
drown me in your raspberry oceans.
Stars stretch out before us like dreams, lost and distant.
Night ripe with promise.
Tomorrow, a child growing in Midnight's blue womb.
Gasping warmth in this chill.
We die, we breathe again.
Broken completely,
Completely broken.

Room at the Edge of the World

Stardust encrusted bones
cast out and pulled in.
On moonbeam music
we spin and collide.

Forever choking through the ages
as our sages falter one by one.
Born under the gun
waiting on heroes and angels.
How long 'till we see this is no fairytale, no fable?

Enough?

Should she sweep stardust off of her boots,
casually proclaiming,
"Bring me wild honey and dewdrops";
Should she dream of windswept plains and bear secret
pains;
Should she hang the moon and swoon galaxies
Would it be enough for you?
Should she walk calmly into the center of your
hurricane,
Should she braid the wind, calm the seas, and hold you
in the mouth of passion;
Would you be unafraid?

On Angels

Of course I believe in angels,
for a million sainted stories I could tell
of light that swells and expels
lurking shadows,
of feathered wings giving shelter while dark demons
sing.
Oh, those grand and mortal souls,
ever daring presence in our nights.

Magic Mirror

Loneliness lay bare her crystal soul.
Dare we peer inside,
discovering desperate dreaming untold?

Reflected refraction dividing and uniting disparate
factions
buried beneath glittering mechanical distractions.
Emasculated hearts exposed,
playing passé parts in Life's passion play.
Secretly dreading the silent dawning day.
Clutching complacent comfort.

Fearing the nearing of truth,
as Plexiglas illusions crackle and melt
in the heat of her desert sweltering.

Autumn's Secret

Autumn's secret, profound wisdom shedding
Man's foolishness betting
conquest may add one drop to a container preordained.

Autumn, humble, remains speechless,
many golden hued treasures flutter softly to the ground,
lifeless,
yet somehow wisdom remains.

Clumsily we grasp at life in desperation,
ever afraid of the vicious sickle.
The preacher cries of salvation,
of death and carnal starvation.

We groan underneath the weight,
shiny things, important things
Life, never one step closer.
Life, Never one step further.

Autumn, that beautiful sage,
Death's Dirge sings.
Majestic truth beheld,
lets her feathers fall without rage.
The secret she has held, life is dying and you would be
right to do it well.

Perfection, Painted Whore

Perfection sits with ruby lips,
and seductive hips,
a light guiding seafaring travelers to rocky waters,
and cold dark graves.
Perfection, thorny mistress,
beacon of the abyss.
Painted whore,
in her cellophane dress.
She peddles illusions,
only affirming delusions,
always alluding to some other place.
Perfection, aloof,
assumes that the errors in our crazy existence are flaws.

I am bold in my mistakes,
content in brokenness.
Only there, am I truly whole.

A Schism

Little notes left
folded neatly and forgotten –
lingering clues.
He stares through me.
Helplessly, I avert.
Nervous
Nauseous
Projecting
Purposeful
We stare,
wanting to know
what it means.
Which one winds gears behind latent fears?
Which one wields unyielding dreams?

Bring Whiskey

Taste the fruit of the earth!
Hacked and hewn,
split and ripped,
Charred and pressed into the cooper's rings.
Here they sing songs of mirth and longing,
dreaming and drowning until the distilling day.

Whether you should come on wings of night,
or in daytime fiery flight —
Death, bring whiskey when you come.
Not rotgut, not rum!
Silken honeyed bourbon,
alive with the flavors of a withering tribe.

Personification of Love's Tragedy

Regret set sail on a sea called hope.
Love, the unwitting stowaway,
sleeps starry eyed dreams,
listening to the wind
gently whispering Youth's foolish promises.

Despair is on the shore,
he never learned to swim.

Indifference stamps out cigarettes like a machine,
laughing, from the quartermaster's chambers

Contentment walks slack-eyed,
surrounded by sharks in suits,
too stupid to know the danger.

When the cutting is done,
Mercy walks him to the place where
Death waits with Innocence, who is always the first
victim.

How I Would Love to Drown

How I would love to drown
current sorrows
in love profound,

That, I know, can never be
until I learn to swim
the resounding deep, complete.

When You Go

In the moment when the reality of your departure
blossoms completely,
echoes of fleeting moments strike me.
I am caught between remembering and coping.

I swear I can almost see you smiling,
but I know you are going in a flurry of brake-lights,
hurried goodbyes,
and welcoming arms.

        (mine are empty)

Loneliness crashes into me,
and rises like the tide-
spilling from my eyes.

Little things shout fading joys;
I am moved by every scrap.
I move nothing.

Shiftless Tides

The sea is formless,
stretching out infinitely before me.
I wonder if this is a good place to let go.
It is useless though,
the tears have barbs,
they refuse to be expelled unless something swells
Are you drowning too?
See I still think of you and smile too.

Highway Hum

There is darkness at the edge, dancing.
Time pools at our feet.
Circumstance stringing
blue blurred lines,
pulled taught between
Reality's dream
and Tomorrow's consequence.

It is raining stingy salty tears.
The highway hums lonely tunes and watches.
It never sleeps,
never remembers.
Here we pray for amnesia from the sins we have seen,
and absolution from the sins we have planned.

Escape

I imagine trapdoors and secret latches.
Reality, a most dreary experience,
leaves me wild-eyed and curious about the other side of
the fence.
A splash of insanity would not be enough.
Give me the whole cup!

Gentle Bird

Sing your song gentle bird
though I know not the word.

Sing your line sublime
as we try to summon time.

Gather it with nets.
Past, Present, and that which has not happened yet.

Ticking transpired
moments expired.

Sing your song gentle bird
though I know not the word.

My world begat,
suspended between hope and regret.

Dreamer

Dreamer, sweet dreamer,
careful with this clock.
Gentle as not to stop the time of all worlds.
Have a long ride.
Dreamer, sweet dreamer,
Have a slice of beauty.
Everything is a warm embrace,
living in love with life.
Everything is a cruel trace of what you must never
become.
Dreamer, sweet dreamer,
take the contents of our frayed minds,
yes mine.
Cast them into the four winds,
and begin anew!

(we called it love)

I have
a hand full
a heart full
of fear.

You call and none of the answers are clear.

I say nothing.
I have plucked the words I held for you.
One by one,
right out of my brain.
One by one,
I have nailed them to these pages.

Maybe I was a violin,
weeping as you pulled desperation's bow
'cross my needy strings.
(we called it love)
Old strings that had forgotten how to sing.
(we called it love)

Sadness has a Sweetness

Sadness has sweetness in it.
Muscle memory of a caress

Sadness has sweetness in it
Sunny days and her whimsical ways,
Preciousness and pain.

Hard to look away
like a soft right into a brick wall,
or the feeling of leaving a world you knew.

Oh, Holy melancholy
remind me of what I have left, lost, or given.
Beautiful nostalgia,
that persistent illusion glorified.

Oh, Holy melancholy
remind me of better days and prices paid.

Come Get Your Claws into Me

The vigor of summer departed
The peace of autumn unfounded
Winter,come get your claws into me.
Icy profound
Those foolish dreams of love, grounded.

Pale faced goddess
sucking on a cigarette
through tight fisted lips.
Desolation without redress.

Winter, come get your claws into me,
this fiery effigy,
a burning man fallen,
reeling drunk – reveling in your misery.
Steel this maddened mind
with your frozen dawn.

Winter austere,
your kiss – your caress,
shivering icy knives,
remove this beating thing from my chest.

Missing You

The hollow of your absence
keeps me awake.
Thoughts of where you might be
visit like phantoms in the night –
always just out of reach,
ever-present, nonetheless.
This is the Gauntlet,
where they take you apart one word at a time.
This is the moment
where I cannot stand, but must not fall.
I will keep digging through the hollow of your absence,
keep kicking through walls
and running through the halls where I always used to
find you.
Spinning wheels and slowly losing my mind
Nothing to do but feel the love, the hollow, the fear, and
the anger
This profound ache that shakes me to the core
this loneliness smiling, mouth open wide,
swallows me whole.

Willow in the Wind

Willow in the wind,
when did winter begin?
Frozen feet and cracked skin.

My water runs freely to the ground.
Willow in the wind, stretch your sagging limbs,
pierce this January sky.

Wooded Icarus,
beat your somber wings,
wrap your roots deep into the sleeping earth,
and pull us into the sun.

Restrained

He smiled,
admired the leash
laughed,
came up from underneath.
I held it in his hands.

He eats words,
scrapes me from me
in jagged pieces.

I am broken,
spilling out.
Could I drop the cord?
Would he paint me across the sky?

Dissonance

Hung like notes on the air
not fluttering or falling,
Just suspended there.

These feet are tired of running,
this heart full of longing.
Winter is near, I pray for spring

A head full of promises
I could not keep.
A handful of dreams,
just let me sleep.

If I could Tell You

You should know,
I sleep holding your blanket.
I cry at the worst times.
I carried your picture at the hearing,
I cried, I showed my sadness, my indignance.

You should know
that I am terrified.
I wish I could put this into words,
but today they all seem small.

You should know
that in some small way
I am you and you are me;
that nothing could ever keep me away.

In your absence
I have wept as a child weeps,
without pride.
I kiss your pictures and dream of you.
You should know,
I carried your picture at the hearing,
I cried, I was indignant.
You were my rock, you should know, but you are only
four.

Untitled 1/24/2014 (For My Kids)

She chases butterflies and moonbeams.
She has pockets full of dreams.

When I look at her,
I know it isn't as hard as it seems.
We talk and she tells me things.

He smiles and follows his heart, wherever it may lead.
I pray he never knows the dark side of need.

When he smiles,
I'll just sit for a while
drinking it in.
I know he will walk upon the wind.

When night crashes in and I am alone again,
I can't help but wonder when
I'll see them walking out in that old warrior's storm.
I can't help but wonder when
I'll see them burn their love into this old world.

Sweet Oblivion

Sweet Oblivion open your arms,
welcome this world weary miscreant,
I have seen too much,
felt too much,
been too much.
Drown this troubled mind in your nothing ambrosia.

Somewhere inside tomorrow reside
all desires, all disappointment.

Oh, you sweet formless lady,
submerge me in Lethe's waters.
Forgetting is beautiful release.
Time's wrinkled plan
ironed smooth,
wiped clean.
Sweet Oblivion, hold me as we begin to dream.

We Put Last Year to Bed

This year we put last year to bed,
soon she will sleep no more.
We watched with storied eyes.
She was dizzy from the weight of many things,
a phoenix with hummingbird wings.

This year we put last year to bed.
We sang her dirge with notes of lead and tears of gold,
released from fear and dread.

This year we put last year to bed.
We laid her in the rustic ground where naught dare
tread.
Only then with whispers and verse,
we dared to dream again.

This year we put last year to bed.

Presently

For it is upon us heavily to love presently.
Diverse mystery reveals itself to us.
Not in acts or miles, but in minutes and years.

Time neither hurries nor dallies, a steady hand that measures
and tallies. It is upon us heavily to love presently.

Yes, there are those that make much show of all they know.
Yet for all their pondering and pontificating
there be but more questioning.

They grumble and mumble,
life they say is for the nimble and the humble.

Oh, those drunken fools who try and understand the
workman by contemplating his tools.

Life is and is not humble or nimble.
'Tis but for living, at the beginning and the end, and it
is upon us heavily to live presently.

Before Leaving

So, where are we now?
Here again in the space between
worlds and dreams
and the reality of your absence.

I am sacrificed on your altar,
you lay sleeping.
I imagine golden fields and expanses.

I am disappearing one second at a time;
you sleep the sleep of the dead.

Spinning

Calm in the center,
my world is spinning one million miles an hour.
Let this evening wash over me.

It is calm in the center as we spin,
forgetting to worry about what holds us together.

The edge is out of control,
but it is calm in my center.
What am I;
A hurricane, tragedy, or another star-crossed traveler?

Just let it ride,
tomorrow it can all fall apart.
Right now, let's just drink this tranquil afternoon

Today, I Release You

I stand before and in the twilight.
Isn't that us,
perpetually trapped between the dark and the light,
too far from the dawn and too close to the night?

Today, I release you.
Today, I seek you.

I was waiting for tomorrow,
running from yesterday.
Just then you caught me up in your silky sweet grace.

Today, I release you.
Today, I beseech you,
do me no kindness,
no mercy.

Let me feel this.
Let me try and understand
loss and longing.
Today, I release you.
Today, I beseech you

Sad Puppets

The seers of things
weep with the sadness it brings.

Knowledge is fine,
sympathy most heavy on the heart

Watching sad puppets in a line,
this one pulls strings
while this one just sits and sings.

Sad puppets crying for drink
and bread to be fed,
for work —
maybe even a whole day's worth.

We are the Struggle

But we are the struggle,
every moment ready to burst forth
in a springing of potential.

We bear solitary burdens
awkward and cumbersome
sprinkled with hope and betrayal.

As the fading sun wrestles impeding night.
As the seedling forces itself through sleeping dirt.

We are the struggle,
pushing on in the face of madness and poverty.
We dare no dream of perfect summer sweet,
'tis the bitter winter night that best illumines our
plight –

For the summer grows hot and lazy,
yet winter, emaciated, fights and waits.

Grey is a Verb

I am scared of disappearing.
This fog descends.
I don't want to make amends.
Just play the chips where they fall.

I stand tall against the night,
these days I ain't sure what's wrong and what's right.

I know I want to love you
like a meteor burning 'cross the night.
I know I want to give my heart,
and not feel like I am dying.

This is my song played in minor keys.
These are my arms, so full of need.

I have stitched all of my broken pieces,
washed the blood with tears,
danced with all my fears.
I know I don't want to disappear.

These days all fade to grey.
All I want is to hold a hurricane.
All I want is to love,
and you to feel the same.

Bag of Bones

You come over the hill
with a smile and a bag of skulls,
said you've been looking for me.

You come over the hill with a smile and a bag of skulls,
and I know it's been a long time.

Here you come girl,
draggin' that bag of bones
and I know I've got to get on home.
I've got to be getting on–
getting on alone.

Vanishing Man

*That road cannot take you anywhere you are not ready
to go.*

I close my eyes and dream.
I have let go,
and I just want you to know
I am a vanishing man.
Yesterday I was here
tomorrow I will disappear.

I have seen the guilt and sadness,
but when the madness gets too heavy
I just brush the sleep out of my eyes
and fade into the wind.

Turning

Some days it seems I have been running all my life,
trying to stop from turning.

Been near and far
Been up and down
Been through Hell,
and I can tell you
it is not what they told you.

Ain't been to heaven yet,
but I am getting closer now.

All these miles come screaming back at me,
their vengeful daggers drawn.
I think I am finally turning away from
the road– into me.

Ain't been to heaven yet,
but I am getting closer now